Classic Tales from Different Cultures

CW00719775

Selected by Roy Blatchford

Contents

Longman

Edinburgh Gate
Harlow, Essex

The Boy Who Cried Wolf

To begin with, the boy liked looking after the sheep. He played all day, and no one stopped him and told him to feed the chickens or gather the eggs or chop the wood. He blew on his whistle and danced with the lambs as they frisked and skipped in the long, lush grass. He scratched his dog's head and threw sticks for her to chase. In the evenings he and the dog drove the flock across the hill to meet up with the other shepherds, and they lay down together beside a roaring fire to sleep.

After a while, however, the boy grew bored.

"It's no FUN up here on my own," he grumbled. "There's no one to talk to. No one takes any notice of me. All the sheep do is chew, chew, chew …" He blew a sad little tune on his pipe. "Even the lambs are too big to dance any more. And there's no sign of a fox or a wolf or a big brown bear …"

The boy stopped. He looked at the sheep grazing quietly among the summer flowers. He looked at his dog dozing in the sunshine. He looked away to where the other shepherds were sitting peacefully with their flocks. He looked down at the little village in the hollow of the hill beneath him. Men and women and children were moving calmly and slowly about their work.

"It's all so DULL," said the boy. "So DULL!" And he jumped to his feet. The sheep raised their heads. The dog opened her eyes.

"WOOOOOOOOOOOOOOOOOOOOOOOOLF!" yelled the boy at the top of his voice.

3

"WOOOOOOOOOOOOOOOOOOOOOOOOLF! HELP! HELP!"
And he ran round and round and in and out of the sheep until they
were all scurrying this way and that in fright.
"BAAAAAAAAAAAAH!" they bleated. "BAAAAAAAAAAAAH!"

The dog barked loudly, and the nearby shepherds snatched at their
sticks and came hurrying to help him. Down in the village everybody
dropped what they were doing and came streaming up the hill.

"Where is it?" they asked. "Where's the wolf? Is it big? Is it fierce?
Has it taken any sheep?" The boy leaned on his stick.
"I drove it away!" he said. "It was huge and grey and hungry, but I
drove it away!"

Everybody cheered. The boy was hugged and fussed and patted and

petted, and the next day his older brother stayed with him. But after that the brother went back to the village, and the boy was left alone again. He sighed as he saw his brother vanish away down the hill.

"That was fun," he said. The boy looked after his sheep for another week. He whistled his tunes, and he threw sticks for his dog, but he did not feel like playing and dancing.

"It's so DULL," he said, and he rubbed his nose and thought.

"H'm," he said and looked around. There were the shepherds tending their sheep, and the people of the village working below, just as they always were.

"WOOOOOOOOOOOOOOOOOOOOOOOLF!" shouted the boy, and he clapped his hands so that the startled sheep hustled and bustled against each other.

"WOOOOOOOOOOOOOOOOOOOOOOOLF!"

The sheep bleated loudly. The dog barked. The shepherds came running. The people of the village hurried up the steep path puffing and panting.

"Where is it? Where's the wolf?" they shouted. The boy shook his head.

"It must have slipped away when it heard you," he said.

The people and the shepherds looked at each other, and several shook their heads. The boy was hugged and told he was brave, but no one stayed with him. Quite soon he was alone again on the hill. "Come on," he said crossly to his dog. "Let's round up the sheep."

The boy looked after his sheep for another three days. He didn't play his whistle, and he hardly spoke to his dog.

"Sheep are dull," he said. "Everything's DULL." The dog wagged her tail, but the boy took no notice.
"Let's have some FUN," he said, and he jumped to his feet.
"WOOOOOOOOOOOOOOOOOOOOOOOOOOOLF!" he shouted.
"WOOOOOOOOOOOOOOOOOOOOOOOOOOLF!"

Even the sheep hardly moved. The dog got slowly to her feet, and a couple of the shepherds came running. A few villagers puffed up the path, but they didn't seem surprised when the boy explained that the HUGE wolf had already vanished. They nodded, and winked at each other before they went back home.

That evening the sky was heavy with dark grey clouds. The boy was thinking it was time to move his sheep across the hill when the dog suddenly began to growl. He looked at her, surprised, and saw that her fur was bristling and her teeth were bared.

"What is it, Dog?" he asked. The sheep were moving restlessly.

"BAAAAAH!" they bleated anxiously. "BAAAAAAAAAAAAH!" And then the boy saw it. A slinking, sliding grey shadow, creeping and crouching as it slipped nearer and nearer.
"WOOOOOOOOOOOOOOOOOOOOOOOOLF!" he yelled. .
"WOOOOOOOOOOOOOOOOOOOOOOLF!"

No one came. They boy yelled again, and again, and again. The dog growled one last growl, and then whimpered and scampered away, her tail between her legs.

"WOOOOOOOOOOOOOOOOOOOOOOOOLF!" the boy screamed and screeched, but still no one answered. With a loud wail he ran for the nearest tree and heaved himself up.

The wolf sprang.

By morning there were no sheep left. Only the boy, sitting in his

tree. When the shepherds came to see why he hadn't come to the fire the night before they saw what had happened.

"I'll never cry wolf again!" the boy sobbed.
"No," said the shepherds, "you won't." And they sent him back down to the village, where he fed the chickens and gathered the eggs and chopped the wood … and never had time to play.

**From *Aesop's Funky Fables*
by Vivian French**

The Old Grandfather and His Grandson

There was once a very old man whose eyes were dim, whose knees tottered under him when he walked, and who was very deaf. As he sat at table, his hand shook so that he would often spill the soup over the table-cloth, or on his clothes, and sometimes even he could not keep it in his mouth when it got there. His son and daughter-in-law were so annoyed at this, that they placed a chair for him in a corner behind the screen, and gave him his meals in an earthenware basin. He would often look sorrowfully at the table with tears in his eyes.

One day the earthenware basin, which he could scarcely hold in his trembling hands, fell to the ground and was broken. The young wife scolded him well for being so careless, but he did not reply, only sighed deeply. Then she bought him a wooden bowl for a few pence, and gave him his meals in it.

They were once sitting thus, when they saw their little boy of four years old sitting at the table and fastening some pieces of wood together.

"What are you making, my boy?" asked his father.
"I am making a little bowl for papa and mamma to eat their food in when I grow up," he replied.

The husband and wife looked at each other without speaking for some minutes. At last they began to shed tears, and went and brought their old father back to the table, and from that day he always took his meals with them, and was never again treated unkindly.

From *Fairytales*
by the Brothers Grimm

The Enchanted Apple-tree

Once upon a time there lived an old woman whose name was Misery.

Her one and only possession was an apple-tree and even this caused her more pain than pleasure. When the apples were ripe, the village urchins came and stole them off the tree. This went on year after year, when one day an old man, with a long white beard, knocked at Misery's door.

"Old woman," he begged, "give me a crust of bread."
"You, too, are a poor miserable creature," said Misery, who although she had nothing herself, was full of compassion for others. "Here is half a loaf, take it; it is all I have, eat it in peace, and may it refresh you."
"As you have been so kind," said the old fellow, "I will grant you a wish."
"Oh!" sighed the old woman, "I have only one desire, that is, that anyone who touches my apple-tree may stick to it until I set them free. The way my apples are stolen from me is past all bearing."

"Your wish is granted," said the old fellow, and he went away.

Two days later Misery went to look at her tree; she found hanging and sticking to the branches a crowd of children, servants, mothers who had come to rescue their children, fathers who had tried to save their wives, two parrots who had escaped from their cage, a cock, a goose, an owl, and other birds, not to mention a goat. When she saw this extraordinary sight, she burst out laughing, and rubbed her hands with delight. She let them all remain hanging on the tree some time before she released them.

The thieves had learnt their lesson, and never stole the apples again.

Some time passed by, when one day someone again knocked at old Misery's door.

"Come in," she cried.

"Guess who I am," said a voice. "I am old Father Death himself.
Listen, little mother," he continued. "I think that you and your old dog
have lived long enough; I have come to fetch you both."

"You are all-powerful," said Misery. "I do not oppose your will, but
before I pack up, grant me one favour. On the tree yonder there grow
the most delicious apples you have ever tasted. Don't you think it
would be a pity to leave them, without gathering one?"

"As you ask me so graciously, I will take one," said Death, whose
mouth was watering as he walked towards the tree.

He climbed up to the topmost branches to gather a large rosy apple, but
directly he touched it, the wretch remained glued to the tree by his long
bony hand. Nothing could tear him off, in spite of his struggles.

"There you are, old tyrant, hanging high and dry," said Misery.

As a result of Death hanging on
the tree, no one died. If persons fell into the
water they were not drowned; if a cart ran over
them they did not even notice it; they did not die even if
their heads were cut off.

After Death had hung, winter and summer, for ten long years on the
tree, through all weathers, the old woman had pity on him, and
allowed him to come down on condition that she should live as long
as she liked.

This Father Death agreed to, and that is why men live longer than
the sparrow, and why Misery is always to be found in the world, and
will doubtless remain until the end of time.

Traditional

The Pleiades

There was once a man and he had six sons. He did not give them, however, any names such as other people have, but called them according to their age, the Oldest, Next to the Oldest, the Next to the Next to the Oldest, the Next to the Next to the Youngest, the Next to the Youngest and the Youngest.

When the Oldest was eighteen and the Youngest twelve, their father sent them out into the world that each might learn a trade. They went together for a short distance until they came to a place where six roads diverged; there they separated and each was to go his own way. But before parting they agreed to meet in two years at that same place and to return to their father together.

On the day appointed they all met and went home to their father who asked each one what he had learned. The Oldest said that he was a shipbuilder and could build ships which could propel themselves. The Next to the Oldest had gone to sea and had become a helmsman and could steer a ship over land as well as over water. The Next to the Next to the Oldest had only learned to listen, but that he could do so well that when he was in one country he could hear what was going on in another. The Next to the Next to the Youngest had become a sharpshooter, and he never missed his aim. The Next to the Youngest had learned how to climb, and he could climb up a wall like a fly and no cliff was too steep for him to scale.

When the father had heard what the five brothers could do, he said
that it was all very well but that he had expected something more
from them. Then he asked what the Youngest had learned; he had
great hopes in him for he was his favourite. The Youngest was glad
that it was at last his turn to speak, and he answered joyously that he
had become a master-thief. When his father heard that he was
furious and exclaimed, "Shame on you, for the disgrace that you
have brought upon me and the whole family."

Now it happened that at this very time the king's beautiful young
daughter had been stolen by a wicked wizard, and the king promised
the half of his realm and the princess in marriage to the one who
should free her from the wizard. When the six brothers heard this
they resolved to try their luck. The shipbuilder built a ship that went

of itself. The helmsman steered it over land and sea. The listener listened carefully and at last said that he heard the wizard inside a mountain of glass. Thither they sailed. The climber quickly climbed to the top of the mountain and saw the ugly wizard lying sleeping with his head in the lap of the princess. Then he hurried down, and taking the little master-thief on his back, went into the inside of the mountain. The thief stole the princess so cleverly from under the head of the wizard that he did not notice it, but continued to sleep.

As soon as they were on board, the ship sailed away, but the listener had to continue to keep a watch on the wizard. When they were not far from land he said to the others, "Now the wizard is awaking! Now he is stretching himself! Now he misses the princess! Now he is coming!"

Now the king's daughter was beside herself with fear, and declared that they would all die if there were not a sharpshooter on board. The wizard could fly through the air and would soon overtake them; he was also invulnerable except in one small black spot, not larger than a pinhead, in the middle of his chest. Hardly had she finished speaking when she saw the wizard in the distance rushing through the air. The sharpshooter took careful aim, shot, and his bullet struck the little black spot and at once the wizard burst into thousands of fiery pieces, and these we know as meteorites.

At last the six brothers reached home with the princess and brought her to the king. But they were all in love with her, and each one could truthfully say that without his help she could not have been saved. Then the king was distressed, for he did not know to whom he should give his daughter. And the princess was also sad, for she did not know whom she loved best.

But God would not that there should be strife among them, so he sent death to the six brothers and to the king's daughter in one and the same night. Then he made of the seven a constellation which men call the Pleiades. And of these stars the brightest is the princess and the faintest the little master-thief.

Traditional

The Conceited Man

Li Chao developed an interest in martial arts as a boy and had a full collection of weapons, such as the stick, broadsword, spear, sword and halberd.

In his spare time, Li Chao would invite friends and neighbours to spar with him. Since he had no teacher to instruct him, his martial arts skills were not very high, even though he possessed extraordinary physical strength.

One day when Li Chao and his friends were boxing, they heard someone shout, "Your bravery is admirable, but it's a pity that your skills are so shallow."

Hearing this, Li Chao could not help flaring up. He looked up and found a monk standing under a tree and smiling at him. Li Chao dashed over to the monk to punch him.

The monk calmly dodged his assault and stroked him on the back. The blow sent him staggering to the ground.

The monk laughed and said, "You have a few more years of learning!" Li Chao blushed.

Li Chao got up and approached the monk. He bowed to him, taking him as his teacher. Moved by his sincerity, the monk readily agreed to receive him.

From then on, Li Chao was absorbed in learning and practising martial arts skills under the monk's instruction. Three months later, Li Chao had made great progress and was often praised by his friends. He grew complacent again.

One day, the monk purposely asked him about his martial arts knowledge.

Li Chao laughed and said, "What the master knows, I know. What the master doesn't know, I also have a smattering of."

When the monk asked Li Chao to display his skills, Li Chao showed everything to his master. After that, Li Chao leapt over to the monk and said loudly, "Master, your disciple's skill is perfect, isn't it?" The monk was silent.

Li Chao thought he had mastered every skill and began to grow lazy. Every day he would stay in bed until noon.

The monk often tried to persuade him to change his ways, but to no avail. Before long, the monk said good-bye to him and went away.

After the monk left, Li Chao issued an open challenge to show off his skills. More than ten days passed, but nobody took up the challenge. Li Chao was bored.

Li Chao set out for the provincial capital immediately upon hearing that there were many able fighters there. Li Chao wandered in the capital for several days, but to his disappointment, did not encounter a single worthy opponent.

One day, Li Chao found many people gathered at a crossroads. He joined the crowd and saw a girl of seventeen or so performing boxing. After the performance, the girl shouted to the audience, "It's so boring to perform alone. Would anyone like to try his hand?"

Three people took up her challenge, but all were beaten by the girl. The audience praised her for her highly skilled martial arts.

Li Chao rushed over, intending to compete with the girl. Without saying a word, the girl met the attack of the fierce new challenger.

After the first round, the girl suddenly stopped and asked, "Would you please tell me who your master is?"
"Why do you ask about my master?" said Li Chao. But as the girl kept questioning, he had to tell her his master's name.

Having heard the name, the girl raised her cupped hands and said, "I admit my defeat. Let's stop here." But Li Chao insisted on continuing. The girl had to go on fighting with Li Chao, who was eager to make a name for himself in the provincial capital by defeating his opponent.

The girl stopped again and said, "We are of one family and it's quite enough to get the general idea with a simple competition."

Thinking that the girl might be scared, Li Chao punched her unawares, but the girl adroitly dodged his blow. Anxious to gain victory, Li Chao pressed forward steadily. The girl had no choice but to meet his attack. With all of his strength, Li Chao tried to punch the girl on the head. She lowered her head and chopped him on the leg. Li Chao tumbled to the ground. With her cupped hands before her chest, the girl apologised, "Sorry for the offence," and stalked off.

Li Chao was sent home by some of the onlookers. A month passed before the wound on his leg healed.

One day as Li Chao was sitting alone, the monk came in. Li Chao told the monk how he had taken a beating.

The monk said, "The girl is my fellow student. It's lucky you gave my name. Otherwise your leg would have been broken."
Taking the monk's hands, Li Chao said to him, "Master, now I understand that however strong you are, there is always someone stronger."

Traditional

The Blind Man

A man carrying a small red box in one hand walked slowly down the street. His old straw hat and faded garments looked as if the rain had often beaten upon them, and the sun had as many times dried them upon his person. He was not old, but he seemed feeble; and he walked in the sun, along the blistering asphalt pavement. On the opposite side of the street there were trees that threw a thick and pleasant shade: people were all walking on that side. But the man did not know, for he was blind, and moreover he was stupid.

In the red box were lead pencils, which he was endeavouring to sell. He carried no stick, but guided himself by trailing his foot along the stone copings or his hand along the iron railings. When he came to the steps of a house he would mount them. Sometimes, after reaching the door with great difficulty, he could not find the electric button, whereupon he would patiently descend and go his way. Some of the iron gates were locked, their owners being away for the summer, and he would consume much time striving to open them, which made little difference, as he had all the time there was at his disposal.

At times he succeeded in finding the electric button: but the man or maid who answered the bell needed no pencil, nor could they be induced to disturb the mistress of the house about so small a thing.

The man had been out long and had walked far, but had sold nothing. That morning someone who had finally grown tired of having him hanging around had equipped him with this box of pencils, and sent him out to make his living. Hunger, with sharp fangs, was gnawing at his stomach and a consuming thirst parched his mouth and tortured him. The sun was broiling. He wore too much clothing – a vest and coat over his shirt. He might have removed these and carried them on his arm or thrown them away; but he did not think of it. A kind woman who saw him from an upper window felt sorry for him, and wished that he would cross over into the shade.

The man drifted into a side street, where there was a group of noisy, excited children at play. The colour of the box which he carried

attracted them and they wanted to know what was in it. One of them
attempted to take it away from him. With the instinct to protect his
own and his only means of sustenance, he resisted, shouted at the
children and called them names. A policeman coming round the
corner and seeing that he was the centre of a disturbance, jerked him

violently around by the collar; but upon perceiving that he was blind, considerably refrained from clubbing him and sent him on his way. He walked on in the sun.

During his aimless rambling he turned into a street where there were monster electric cars thundering up and down, clanging wild bells and literally shaking the ground beneath his feet with their terrific impetus. He started to cross the street.

Then something happened – something horrible happened that made the women faint and the strongest men who saw it grow sick and dizzy. The motorman's lips were as grey as his face, and that was ashen grey; and he shook and staggered from the superhuman effort he had put forth to stop his car.

Where could the crowds have come from so suddenly, as if by magic? Boys on the run, men and women tearing up on their wheels to see the sickening sight: doctors dashing up in buggies as if directed by Providence.

And the horror grew when the multitude recognised in the dead and mangled figure one of the wealthiest, most useful and most influential men of the town, a man noted for his prudence and foresight. How could such a terrible fate have overtaken him? He was hastening from his business house, for he was late, to join his family, who were to start in an hour or two for their summer home on the Atlantic coast. In his hurry he did not perceive the other car coming from the opposite direction, and the common, harrowing thing was repeated.

The blind man did not know what the commotion was all about. He had crossed the street, and there he was, stumbling on in the sun, trailing his foot along the coping.

**From *Shorties*
by Kate Chopin**

Clever Maggie

There was once a cook named Maggie who had shoes with red heels, and when she went out of doors, she would draw herself up and walk proudly, and say to herself, "I really am a handsome maiden." When she came home she would drink a glass of wine, and as wine and air gave her an appetite, she would eat up all the best things till she was satisfied, and say to herself, "The cook ought to know the taste of everything."

One day her master said to her, "Maggie, I have invited a friend to supper; cook me two chickens."
"That will I do, master," she replied. So she went out and killed two fowls and prepared them for roasting.

In the afternoon she placed them on the spit before the fire, and they were all ready, and beautifully hot, and brown by the proper time, but the visitor had not arrived. So she went to her master, and said, "The fowls will be spoilt if I keep them at the fire any longer. It will be a pity and a shame if they are not eaten soon."

Then said her master, "I will go and fetch the visitor myself," and away he went.

As soon as his back was turned, Maggie put the spit with the birds on one side, and thought, "I have been standing by the fire so long that it has made me quite thirsty. Who knows when they will come? While I am waiting I may as well run into the cellar, and have a little drop." So she seized a jug, and said, "All right, Maggie, thou shalt have a good draught. Wine is so tempting," she said again, "and it does not do to spoil your draught," and then she drank without stopping till the jug was empty.

After this she went into the kitchen, and placed the fowls again before the fire, basted them with butter, and rattled the spit round so that they browned and frizzled with the heat.

"They would never miss a little piece," she said to herself. Then she dipped her finger in the dripping-pan to taste and cried, "Oh, how nice these fowls are! It is a sin and a shame that there is no one here to eat them."

She ran to the window to see if her master and the guest were coming; but she could see no one. So she went and stood again by the fowls, and thought, "The wing of that fowl is a little burnt. I had better eat it." She cut it off, as she thought this, and ate it up, and it tasted so nice that when she had finished it, she thought, "I must have the other. Master will never notice that anything is wanting."

After the two wings were eaten, Maggie again went to look for her master, but there were no signs of his appearance. "Who knows?" she said to herself, "perhaps the visitor is not coming at all, and they have kept my master to supper, so he won't be back."

"Hi! Maggie, there are good things left for you, and that piece of fowl has made me thirsty. I must have another drink before I eat the rest." So she went into the cellar, took a large draught of wine, and, returning to the kitchen, sat down, and ate the remainder of the fowl with great relish.

There was now one fowl gone, and, as her master did not return, Maggie began to look at the other with longing eyes. At last she said, "Where one is, there must the other be; for the fowls belong to each other, and what is right for one is also fair and right for the other. I believe, too, I want some more to drink. It won't hurt me." The last draught gave her courage. She came back to the kitchen, and let the second fowl go after the first.

As she was enjoying the last morsel, home came her master.
"Make haste, Maggie," he cried. "The guest will be here in a few minutes."
"Yes, master," she replied. "It will soon be all ready."

Meanwhile, the master saw that the cloth was laid, and everything in order. So he took up the carving-knife, with which he intended to carve the fowl, and went out to sharpen it on the stones in the passage.

While he was doing so, the guest arrived, and knocked gently and courteously at the house-door. Maggie ran out to see who it was, and when she caught sight of the visitor, she placed her finger on her lips, and whispered, "Hush, hush! Go back again as quickly as you came. If my master should catch you, it would be unfortunate. He did invite you to supper this evening, but with no other intention than to cut off both your ears. Listen, you can hear him sharpening his knife."

The guest heard the sound, and hastened as fast as he could down the steps, and was soon out of sight.

Maggie was not idle. She ran screaming to her master, and cried, "You have invited a fine visitor!"
"Hi! Why, Maggie, what do you mean?"
"Oh!" she exclaimed, "he has taken my two beautiful fowls, and run away with them."

"What strange conduct!" said her master, who was sorry to lose his supper. "If he had left me one, or at least enough for my own supper!" He ran after the guest and called to him to stop. But the more he cried to him, the faster he ran; and when he saw him with the knife in his hand, and heard him say, "Only one! only one!" (he meant, if he had left him "only one fowl"), he thought he spoke of "only one ear," which he intended to cut off, and so he ran as if fire were burning around him, so that he might reach home with both ears untouched.

From *Fairytales*
by the Brothers Grimm

Banjo

Banjo lived and died in obscurity. Born on the street, he died on the street. Found in a garbage bin, his remains now rot in a garbage disposal dump.

He lived for three months, and in that time he made Helen and myself and a few others very happy, and caused no one any pain.

When I found Banjo, he was a weak and wiry little puppy, suspicious of all people, and very afraid of them. His ribs hung down in streaks from his back like banjo strings, and his head, which was all eyes, was ten times too big for his body. It rested precariously on his shoulders, and his ears perched on his head like floppy birds on a branch.

The first time I approached this little brown dog, he scrambled out of the overturned garbage bin, and stumbled, with his tail tucked between his bony legs, and his head turned warily in my direction, under the car, whining. Every time I approached him, he would shift his position cleverly – moving from under one wheel to the other. I knew that he was afraid of me, but he also knew that I was afraid of him. He knew that I did not want to frighten or startle him in my effort to catch him. He knew, I think, that I did not want to chase him away. What he did not understand, was why.

And so, he circled me, and I circled him from bumper to bumper. Eventually, after enticing him with a bowl of milk and stale bread, which he wisely refused, I gave up the chase and went upstairs to the kitchen resigned to the fact that I had been outwitted. Through the window I saw his spindly legs carry him bouncing down the drive and out into the street. Impulsively I ran downstairs after him. He had strolled into the next-door neighbour's yard and was nonchalantly smelling around behind the low entrance wall. I crept closer. He was rustling in the grass behind the wall, occupied, not expecting me to strike back, especially in somebody else's yard. I stepped softly, slowly, crouching slightly behind the wall, with only my head showing. Now we were opposite each other, he on one side of the wall, I on the other. There he was backing me, completely unaware of my presence. Then in a flash, my hands were down upon him. He jumped and tried to wriggle out of my grasp, yelping, his head waving madly, in utter disbelief and confusion.

In the living room of our house there was a large couch which was pushed up against a wall. And it was here that Banjo spent his first week with us. He was very much afraid of his new surroundings, and still very suspicious of our motives. He would sit behind the couch all day without revealing himself and every time we approached him he would shiver all over like a vibrating banjo string.

At first Banjo would eat nothing. We tried bread soaked in milk, and when he refused that, we tried milk and eggs; but he would have none of it. He was so young and starved that we thought we should wean him gradually on to harder food. However, after the first day of trying in vain to get him to eat, we became desperate, thinking that he would die at any moment. That night after dinner, however, our worries came to an end. We had eaten oxtail stew for dinner, and I put the left-over bones on a plate next to the couch, just as a last resort, not thinking him old enough to eat such food. To my surprise, when Banjo thought we were not looking he sneaked out from under the couch, and one by one the bones disappeared into his cave of solitude.

The next morning when I offered him some more bones, I held one in my hand, and pushed it in front of Banjo's nose. He cocked his huge head to one side and eyed me inquiringly. He did not quite understand this macabre game. I wanted him out from behind the couch, he was aware of that much; but he was still too wary of human beings to realise that what I really wanted was to build up some sort of friendly relationship with him.

Hunger, however, makes a fool of a man and dog alike, and eventually he took his first bone, shaking all over, from my hand.

From that moment our relationship developed. By the end of the first week he had ceased to live like a hermit and was walking, however unsteadily, around the house investigating every corner like a determined Sherlock Holmes.

The day soon came when Banjo followed us everywhere we went in the house.

Then the day of decision came. We opened the doors to Banjo for the first time since we had found him. He was free to stay or go. We watched him intently through the kitchen window as he sniffed his way slowly down the drive and contemplated the public road. He turned around, sat down again, and contemplated his surroundings. He looked back at the road outside, wagged his tail, and came pelting up the drive and into the house.

The last time I saw Banjo alive was around 7 o'clock one Sunday evening. We were watching television, and it was not until about one hour later that I really began to worry about him. I thought maybe he was next door.

I walked out into the front yard and whistled and called for him from the gate. But I did not hear the characteristic patter of his tiny feet. I walked out in the street. In the middle of the road lay a dark mass, a shadow.

I knew it was Banjo. I knew too that he was dead. I had never really expected to find him dead. Death was always something separate from life, something distant and fantastic. I bent down beside the body. His hind legs were spraddled out behind him and his body was bloated. There was a large gash along his stomach, not a puncture, but the skin had been ripped off and I saw the black tyre squeezing and pinching the flesh against the tar road. I saw the wheel turning over and the body being sucked under.

The body lay on the road cold and distorted.

I removed the collar from around Banjo's neck and hopelessly began to cry.

**From *West Indian Stories*
by Denis Foster**